D1573330

ULTIMATE SPECIAL FORCES

US ARMY RANGERS

TIM COOKE

PowerKiDS
press.

New York

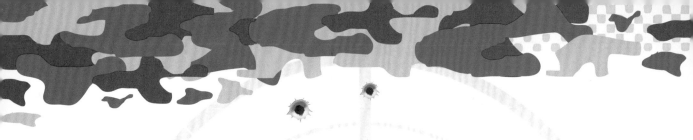

Published in 2013 by The Rosen Publishing Group, Inc.
29 East 21st Street, New York, NY 10010

Senior Editor: Tim Cooke
US Editor: Sara Antill
Designer: Supriya Sahai
Creative Director: Jeni Child
Picture Researcher: Andrew Webb
Picture Manager: Sophie Mortimer
Children's Publisher: Anne O'Daly
Editorial Director: Lindsey Lowe

PICTURE CREDITS
Front Cover: US Army
Cody Images: 21; Getty Images: Scott Peterson 28, 29; Library of Congress: 04, 05, 24, 25tr; Robert Hunt Library: 18, 19, 20, 25br; US Air Force: 10, 38, 39. 43tr; US Army: 06, 07, 08, 09, 12, 13tl, 13b, 16, 17, 34, 35, 36, 44; US Department of Defense: 11, 14, 15, 22, 23, 26, 27, 30, 31, 32, 33, 37, 40, 41, 42, 43bl, 45tr, 45br.
Key: t = top, c = center, b = bottom, l = left, r = right.

Library of Congress Cataloging-in-Publication Data

Cooke, Tim, 1961–
 US Army Rangers / by Tim Cooke.
    p. cm. — (Ultimate special forces)
 Includes index.
 ISBN 978-1-4488-7879-6 (library binding) — ISBN 978-1-4488-7956-4 (pbk.) — ISBN 978-1-4488-7961-8 (6-pack)
 1. United States. Army—Commando troops—Juvenile literature. I. Title.
 UA34.R36C67 2013
 356'.1670973—dc23

                             2012012877

Manufactured in the United States of America

CPSIA Compliance Information: Batch #B2S12PK: For further information, contact Rosen Publishing, New York, New York, at 1-800-237-9932

CONTENTS

INTRODUCTION

The Army Rangers are older than the United States. British colonists used armed men to "range" the countryside for protection. In the French and Indian War (1754–1763) Captain Robert Rogers and his men covered up to 14 miles (22 km) a day on long-range patrols. In 1756, Rogers was asked to set up a "ranging school." His "Rules of Ranging" are still used today. In the American Revolution (1775–1783) Rogers fought on the side of the British.

ROBERT ROGERS introduced many of the tactics still used by the Rangers.

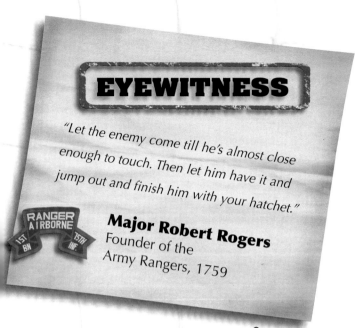

EYEWITNESS

"Let the enemy come till he's almost close enough to touch. Then let him have it and jump out and finish him with your hatchet."

Major Robert Rogers
Founder of the
Army Rangers, 1759

MOSBY'S RANGERS showed how effective a ranger force could be in wartime.

MODERN RANGERS

During the Civil War (1861–1865), the South used Rangers as a form of irregular troops. Mosby's Rangers, led by John S. Mosby, harassed Union forces during the winter of 1863 by carrying out guerrilla attacks in parts of Virginia.

The modern Rangers were created in World War II (1939–1945). General George Marshall ordered the creation of the 1st US Army Ranger Battalion. It was modeled on the British commandos, who were trained to work in small groups to stage raids in enemy territory.

ORGANIZATION

Since their early days, the Rangers have been put together or disbanded as necessary. After the Vietnam War (1964–1975) army chiefs wanted to create an elite force ready to deploy on short notice. In 1974, General Creighton Abrams set up the 1st Ranger Battalion; it was followed by two more battalions. In 1986, the 75th Ranger Regiment was formed as the home for the 1st, 2nd, and 3rd battalions.

THIS SIGN stands outside Ranger headquarters at Fort Benning, in Georgia.

RANGERS HOLD a ceremony to welcome a new commander for the 75th Ranger Regiment.

TRAINING AND INTELLIGENCE

The 4th, 5th, and 6th battalions, meanwhile, were reactivated as the Ranger Training Brigade. Their job is to train new Ranger recruits. Another new battalion was established in 2006. Called the Regimental Special Troops Battalion, it is now responsible for intelligence, reconnaissance, and maintenance missions. There are a total of around 2,000 Army Rangers; their headquarters is at Fort Benning, Georgia.

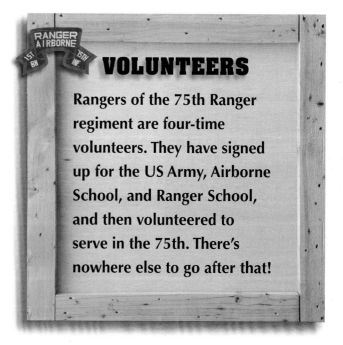

VOLUNTEERS

Rangers of the 75th Ranger regiment are four-time volunteers. They have signed up for the US Army, Airborne School, and Ranger School, and then volunteered to serve in the 75th. There's nowhere else to go after that!

RANGER CREED

Rangers join a unique and small club. They all learn the Ranger Creed, which emphasizes the values by which they live: honor, gallantry, dedication, and strength. The first letter of each phrase spells out the word R-A-N-G-E-R. The creed is so successful that a version of it has been adopted by Ranger units in armies around the world.

RANGERS RECITE the Ranger Creed during an award ceremony.

A RANGER RECRUIT rests after a march in weather cold enough to form an icicle on his helmet.

THE RANGER CREED

Recognizing that I volunteered as a Ranger, fully knowing the hazards of my chosen profession, I will always endeavor to uphold the prestige, honor, and high esprit de corps of my Ranger Regiment.

Acknowledging the fact that a Ranger is a more elite soldier who arrives at the cutting edge of battle by land, sea, or air, I accept the fact that as a Ranger my country expects me to move farther, faster, and fight harder than any other soldier.

Never shall I fail my comrades. I will always keep myself mentally alert, physically strong, and morally straight and I will shoulder more than my share of the task whatever it may be. One-hundred percent and then some.

Gallantly will I show the world that I am a specially selected and well-trained soldier. My courtesy to superior officers, neatness of dress, and care of equipment shall set the example for others to follow.

Energetically will I meet the enemies of my country. I shall defeat them on the field of battle for I am better trained and will fight with all my might. Surrender is not a Ranger word. I will never leave a fallen comrade to fall into the hands of the enemy and under no circumstances will I ever embarrass my country.

Readily will I display the intestinal fortitude required to fight on to the Ranger objective and complete the mission though I be the lone survivor.

INDOCTRINATION

He eing a Ranger is more than being an elite soldier. Rangers share a great pride in their history. They learn Rogers' Rules and live by them. The first stage of training used to be called the Ranger Indoctrination Program (RIP). Since 2011, it has been renamed the Ranger Assessment and Selection Program (RASP). But its purpose is the same. The two parts of the eight-week selection program are designed to make sure that candidates have the mental and physical strength it takes to be a Ranger.

A TRAINEE eats his first hot meal in days while sitting in the rain.

TWO PHASES

In phase one Rangers must run 5 miles (8 km) in under 40 minutes and march 12 miles (20 km) in three hours with a heavy rucksack. They must pass the Ranger Swim Ability Evaluation (RSAE) course. There are also psychological tests to make sure they won't crack under stress. Phase two teaches marksmanship, mobility, and physical fitness. Only candidates who pass both stages of RASP get to wear the tan beret.

EYEWITNESS

"The Ranger Battalion is to be an elite, light, and the most proficient infantry battalion in the world. It must be a battalion that can do things with its hands and weapons better than anyone. Wherever the battalion goes, it will be apparent it is the best."

Gen. Creighton Abrams
U.S. Army Chief of Staff

RANGERS DEMONSTRATE crossing a rope bridge during Indoctrination.

RANGER SCHOOL

Ranger School trains officers. The Ranger Training Brigade oversees a 61-day course that has been called the toughest combat course in the world. It's so tough that members of other US elite units and special forces send their officers to train there, too. The Rangers who go to Ranger School have already passed the Ranger Assessment and Selection Program (RASP) and joined the 75th Ranger Brigade.

PRIZED TAB

Candidates who pass Ranger School are awarded the highly sought-after Ranger tab. Worn on the upper shoulder of the left sleeve, the yellow and black tab spells out RANGER in yellow letters.

IN THE "Walk" phase, soldiers prepare to rappel down a 50-foot-(15 m) tall rockface.

SOLDIERS DOING abdominal kicks as punishment for a minor misdemeanor.

A CANDIDATE crosses a rope bridge in the "Walk" phase.

TOUGHEST IN THE WORLD

The Ranger course has three phases, known as "Crawl," "Walk," and "Run." The "Crawl" phase is held at Fort Benning, Georgia. Candidates have to pass physical tests, like running 2 miles (3.2 km) in under 13 minutes. They learn patrol skills and how to work in small units, all with little sleep or food. Successful recruits learn to "walk" in the mountain phase. They spend 20 days in small units, surviving in harsh conditions. It's freezing cold, there is little food, and no one gets enough sleep. If candidates pass, it's on to the "Run" phase in Florida.

SWAMP TRAINING

The last part of Ranger School is the "Run" phase. It takes place in the wetlands of the Florida panhandle. The Ranger candidates parachute into Camp Rudder, where they spend 18 days learning how to deal with swamp and coastal environments. As before, they get only limited food and sleep (an average of four hours a night). They also have to deal with severe weather and unfamiliar terrain, as well as mental and physical fatigue.

RANGERS UNDERTAKE a 5-mile- (8 km) long hike during the last week of training in Florida.

CANDIDATES APPROACH the "enemy" base during the combat exercise.

SWAMP LIFE

The candidates have to swim through dirty swamp water that is bitterly cold. They carry their heavy packs as they wade up to their waists in creeks. They learn how to cross rivers by rope and get used to using small boats for amphibious operations. They also learn how to deal with venomous snakes, alligators, and other creatures. The biggest part of the course is a nine-day exercise in which the candidates work together in small teams in a realistic and tough combat exercise to capture a stronghold from the "enemy."

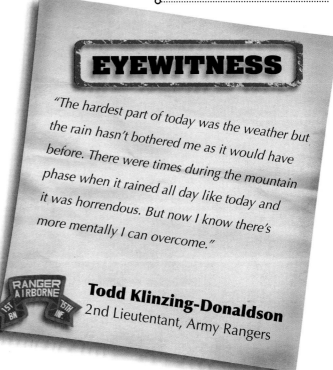

EYEWITNESS

"The hardest part of today was the weather but the rain hasn't bothered me as it would have before. There were times during the mountain phase when it rained all day like today and it was horrendous. But now I know there's more mentally I can overcome."

Todd Klinzing-Donaldson
2nd Lieutenant, Army Rangers

TRAINING

Rangers can be deployed anywhere in the world within 18 hours. They must be combat ready at all times, so they train constantly. Each Ranger has a specific skill, such as sniper shooting, scuba diving, or free-fall parachuting. Rangers train in different conditions, from the Arctic to the tropical forests of the Panama Canal Zone. They are trained for urban, nonurban, desert, and mountain combat. They are ready to go wherever an elite force might be needed.

RANGERS IN full combat gear keep watch during an urban warfare exercise.

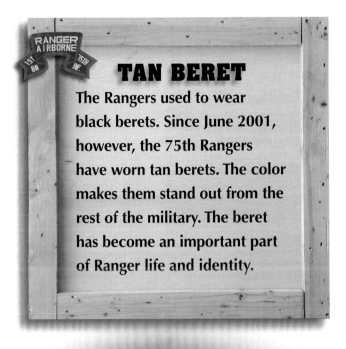

TAN BERET

The Rangers used to wear black berets. Since June 2001, however, the 75th Rangers have worn tan berets. The color makes them stand out from the rest of the military. The beret has become an important part of Ranger life and identity.

RANGE OF SKILLS

All Rangers are trained in infantry skills, such as markmanship, but as advised in Rogers' Rules, they can also fight hand-to-hand if necessary. At Ranger School they plan and carry out daily patrolling, which is vital in a combat situation. They learn how to do reconnaissance, launch ambushes, and raid different targets. That might mean storming a house in a densely populated city to rescue a hostage, or hunting for terrorists in a labyrinth of caves in the mountains of Afghanistan.

RANGERS KEEP their weapons ready during urban training.

WORLD WAR II
EUROPE 1942–1945

RANGERS ROUND up German prisoners at Pointe du Hoc on D-Day.

In 1942 the Rangers were reformed under an outstanding leader, Major William Orlando Darby. Darby's Rangers took part in key operations such as the invasions of North Africa and Sicily. But tragedy struck at Anzio in Italy in January 1944. Three Ranger battalions were lost when an operation went wrong. Only six out of 767 Rangers escaped from the German attack; the rest were either killed or taken prisoner.

RANGERS RECREATE their ascent of the slippery cliffs at Pointe du Hoc, showing how they used rope ladders.

EYEWITNESS

"Foremost in our minds was the challenge of getting up that cliff, which was wet from rain and clay and very slippery. The Germans were shooting down. They were cutting ropes. They were trying to kill us. These guys were positive thinkers. They thought if they got an even chance in a fight they would win."

Sgt. Leonard Lomell
2nd Ranger Battalion,
Pointe du Hoc

POINTE DU HOC

On June 6, 1944, called D-Day, Rangers landed early on the Normandy beaches. Their job was to take out German positions to make it easier for the main Allied landings. The most famous achievement was at Pointe du Hoc, a cliff on Omaha Beach. The 2nd Battalion's mission was to destroy a German strongpoint on the cliff top. They used rope ladders to scale the cliff, but found the strongpoint had been moved. Although under heavy fire, the Rangers held on to the key position. Only 90 of 225 men survived the mission.

WORLD WAR II
PACIFIC 1944–1945

THE ALAMO SCOUTS played a key role in the liberation mission at Cabanatuan.

Although most of the action the Rangers saw in World War II was in Europe, the 6th Ranger Battalion played a key role in the Pacific. The 6th was only formed in September 1944, but it soon saw combat. It led the invasion of Leyte, an island in the Philippines, toward the end of the year. The landings marked the start of the end of Japanese occupation of the Philippines. The 6th Rangers raised the first US flag on Philippine soil in three years.

MAP OF THE PHILIPPINES

US FORCES landed on Leyte to begin the liberation of the Philippines.

POW RESCUE

The most famous mission of the 6th Rangers was a raid to free Allied prisoners of war (POWs) from a Japanese camp in Cabanatuan, 60 miles (95 km) from the capital, Manila. The Rangers trekked through dense jungle to reach the camp. They attacked at dusk on January 30, 1945. Although the camp was defended by 2,000 Japanese soldiers, the Rangers quickly liberated the nearly 500 POWs. The raid is still the most successful rescue operation in US military history.

EYEWITNESS

"No incident of this war has given me greater satisfaction than the Ranger rescue of these Americans."

Douglas MacArthur
General of the US Army, field marshal of the Philippine Army.

MERRILL'S MARAUDERS
trek in Burma, now called Myanmar. The Marauders were based on the Rangers and did a similar job.

KOREA

1950–1953

In 1950, with war looming in Korea, the Rangers were reactivated. They became an airborne force, and made their first combat jump in Korea. From now on, the Rangers would concentrate on small operations. They would act as scouts, gather intelligence, perform raids, catch POWs in ambushes, or form a spearhead for an infantry attack.

MAP OF SOUTH KOREA

NORTH KOREA

Paengnyong

Inch'on Seoul Han

SOUTH KOREA

Yellow Sea Taejon

Kum

Naktong Taegu

Ulsan

Kwangju

Pusan Sea of Japan

Ulung

Tsushima (Japan)

Cheju Korea Strait

JAPAN

THE WAR in Korea ended with the division of the peninsula into North and South Korea.

A RANGER marksman takes aim at the enemy from the cover of a tank.

RANGERS prepare for a night patrol against the enemy in North Korea.

AN ARMY FIRST

The 2nd Ranger Infantry Company (Airborne) was the US Army's first Ranger unit made up of all African Americans. Their mission was to block enemy threats from northeast Korea. The unit won the Bronze Arrowhead for its parachute assault at Munsan-ni.

ON THE GROUND

Six new Ranger battalions served in Korea as special operation units. A company of 112 Rangers would be attached to an infantry division of between 17,000 and 20,000 men. The largest Ranger action was on March 23, 1951. Two Airborne Ranger companies parachuted into Munsan-ni, in the demilitarized zone between North and South Korea, to prevent the retreat of North Korean and Chinese troops from Seoul.

VIETNAM
1963–1973

MAP OF SOUTHEAST ASIA

CHINA

Hanoi · Haiphong

LAOS

Gulf of Tonkin · Hainan (CHINA)

THAILAND

South China Sea

Hue · Da Nang

VIETNAM

CAMBODIA

Nha Trang

Mekong

Ho Chi Minh City

Long Xuyen · Can Tho

Gulf of Thailand

South China Sea

The Rangers were reactivated at the start of the Vietnam War. They formed small units known as Long Range Patrols (LRPs) and Long Range Reconnaissance Patrols (LRRPs). Their job was to carry out reconnaissance and to get behind enemy lines by air, ground, or water. Patrols could gather much better intelligence than aerial photographs; surveillance technology was still in its early days.

A UH-1 "HUEY" hovers to provide air cover for Rangers during a patrol in Vietnam.

EYEWITNESS

"The aerial recons were an exciting time. A critical part of those flights was to locate landing zones for the helicopters. There could be no dead falls, camouflaged pits dug to snare an unsuspecting pilot."

Colonel Robert W. Black
8th Airborne Ranger Company

A RADIO operator calls in air support during a Ranger patrol.

LONG-RANGE PATROLS

When the United States joined the growing conflict in Vietnam, it soon became clear that the military needed special units that could operate behind enemy lines. LRPs were formally set up in late 1967. They were either 118 men attached to a division or 61 men attached to a brigade. From February 1, 1969, the LRPs were called "Rangers" and were attached to the 75th Infantry Regiment. As was the pattern from previous conflicts, these Ranger units were disbanded after the war.

A RANGER sergeant poses for the camera before setting out on a mission in Vietnam in 1970.

CENTRAL AMERICA

1980s

MAP OF PANAMA

Caribbean Sea

COSTA RICA

L. Gatún • Colón · L. Bayano
La Chorrera ■ **Panama City**
David • **PANAMA** • Penonomé
• Santiago
• Las Tablas

Gulf of Panama

COLOMBIA

PACIFIC OCEAN

On December 20, 1989, the entire 75th Ranger battalion—1,500 men—was sent to the Central American country of Panama. Its mission was to prepare the way for ground troops to enter the country. The mission, Operation Just Cause, aimed to remove the military dictator General Manuel Noriega from power.

RANGERS GATHER around a light utility vehicle armed with an M-60 machine gun for a briefing during Operation Urgent Fury.

TASK FORCE RED

Code-named Task Force Red, 500 Rangers made an early morning assault on Panama's international airport. They landed by parachute and quickly overcame Panamanian forces. Another 500 Rangers made a low-level night jump on the military airport, supported by helicopter gunships. Within two hours they had secured the target with a loss of just four men, 27 wounded, and 35 injuries caused by the parachute jump. The Rangers remained in Panama until January 1990 tracking down Noriega's troops. By the time they left, they had taken more than 1,000 enemy soldiers as prisoners.

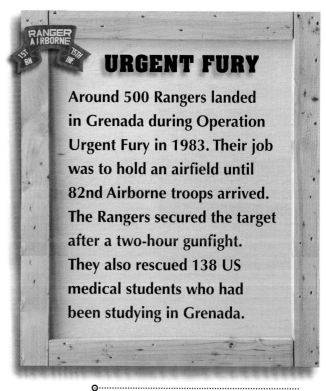

URGENT FURY

Around 500 Rangers landed in Grenada during Operation Urgent Fury in 1983. Their job was to hold an airfield until 82nd Airborne troops arrived. The Rangers secured the target after a two-hour gunfight. They also rescued 138 US medical students who had been studying in Grenada.

1st BATTALION, 75th Rangers, hold a ceremony to mark their return from Panama.

SOMALIA
1993

MAP OF SOMALIA

The Battle of Mogadishu, in Somalia, saw the fiercest ground combat by US forces since the Tet Offensive in Vietnam in 1968. The US disaster in Mogadishu inspired the book and movie *Black Hawk Down*. The story began when 3rd Battalion of the 75th Rangers was sent to Somalia, in the Horn of Africa, to capture a local warlord named Mohammed Farrah Aidid.

RANGERS HAD to get deep into the center of the Somali capital, Mogadishu.

NO MAN LEFT BEHIND

On October 3, Aidid's men shot down a US Black Hawk helicopter. The Rangers went in to help the crew, but were attacked by Aidid's militia. When Rangers tried to rescue the crew of a second Black Hawk that was shot down, they were all killed. The next day the survivors were rescued by their fellow Rangers. The fighting cost the lives of 16 Rangers, but the mission followed the Ranger Creed: no Ranger was left behind.

A BLACK HAWK
lands at a US base during the Battle of Mogadishu.

EYEWITNESS

"How many Rangers were wounded? I had no idea. All I knew was that we were taking fire from every direction and were in a fight for our lives."

Sergeant Matt Eversmann
3rd Battalion, 75th Rangers, Mogadishu

AFGHANISTAN
2001

Soldiers of 3rd Battalion, 75th Rangers were the first US force to set foot on Afghan soil as part of Operation Enduring Freedom. President George Bush had authorized the hunt for the terrorist Osama bin Laden after the attacks of September 11, 2001. Bin Laden was protected by the Taliban regime in Afghanistan. The Rangers would have to hunt for him in mountains and deserts.

MAP OF AFGHANISTAN

1st PLATOON, B Company, 75th Rangers pose in Afghanistan in November 2003.

RANGERS TAKE defensive positions while patrolling an Afghan village.

OBJECTIVE RHINO

On October 19, 2001, 199 Rangers began Objective Rhino. They were dropped by four MC-130 aircraft onto a desert landing strip close to the northern city of Kandahar. With AC-130 Spectre gunships circling overhead, the Rangers quickly secured the landing strip and established a base. Over the following months, Rangers carried out long-range patrols in enemy territory to gather intelligence. They searched caves deep in the Afghan mountains for Osama bin Laden, but had no success.

ANACONDA

More than 2,000 troops took part in Operation Anaconda in March 2002. The task was to root out Taliban and al-Qaeda from the Afghanistan mountains. Special forces were inserted in observation posts to keep watch on the enemy.

AFGHANISTAN

2002

Navy SEALs were to be inserted on the Takur Ghar mountain to set up an observation point. On March 4, 2002, two MH-47 Chinooks tried to land, but were attacked by the Taliban. A Navy SEAL fell out of the helicopter. A Quick Reaction Force went in to rescue him. The enemy attacked the helicopter, Razor 01, which crashed high on the mountain. The Rangers came under heavy fire; three men were killed immediately.

A RANGER SNIPER keeps watch in the mountains of Afghanistan.

RESCUE MISSION

Razor 02 landed lower down the mountain for a new rescue. The Rangers crawled up the steep, snow-covered slope under heavy fire. Seven Rangers stormed to the top, knee-deep in snow. Using grenades and rifle fire, they pushed the Taliban back down the mountain. The Rangers then consolidated their position and moved their wounded and dead to safety. By nightfall, reinforcements had secured the mountaintop. Eight US Special Forces, including three Rangers, had been killed.

RANGERS CONDUCT a house-to-house search in an Afghan village.

EYEWITNESS

"We're searching for a missing American who fell out of a helicopter in enemy territory two hours ago. He is somewhere below us in the Shah-i-Khot Valley, an area teeming with hundreds of al-Qaeda fighters. Right now, there's no place on earth more hostile to US soldiers—and no place my team would rather be. We're here because we are Rangers, and we have a creed to uphold: never leave a fallen comrade."

Captain Nate Self
Commander,
Quick Reaction Force

IRAQ
1991, 2003

MAP OF IRAQ

Operation Desert Storm was the US-led liberation of Kuwait from its neighbor, Iraq, in 1991. Rangers from the 1st Battalion were part of a large-scale ground attack code-named Desert Sabre. They destroyed border observation posts. They also penetrated deep into Iraqi territory to destroy a facility that controlled the launch of Scud missiles. The invasion won a comprehensive victory in just 100 hours.

A RANGER squad keeps watch during a nighttime patrol in Iraq.

A RANGER FROM 2nd Battalion watches from a rooftop during a mission.

BACK TO IRAQ

A second invasion of Iraq followed in 2003 in Operation Iraqi Freedom. On April 1, 2003, Rangers from 3rd Battalion began a mission to seize the Haditha Dam. They had to make sure Iraqi forces could not destroy it, causing floods and damaging the electricity supply. The dam was protected by 200 Iraqi soldiers supported by tanks. As the Rangers penetrated the dam complex, a fierce battle broke out. The two sides fought for six days before the Rangers secured their target.

EYEWITNESS

"On Day Six the artillery began again. This was extremely demoralizing to the platoon. We all were extremely worn out. Dodging artillery rounds all day and digging all night was really starting to take its toll. Only a few rounds came in this day."

Platoon Sergeant
Company B, 3rd Battalion, 75th Rangers

RESCUE IN IRAQ

On March 23, 2003, the US Army private Jessica Lynch was captured by Iraqi forces after the convoy she was traveling in was attacked by insurgents. Lynch's Humvee was hit by a rocket propelled grenade, or RPG. Lynch was the only soldier taken alive. She spent nine days in an Iraqi hospital. When news of her capture leaked out, a rescue mission was launched on April 1, 2003.

RANGERS STORM a building on a night raid to hunt for insurgents.

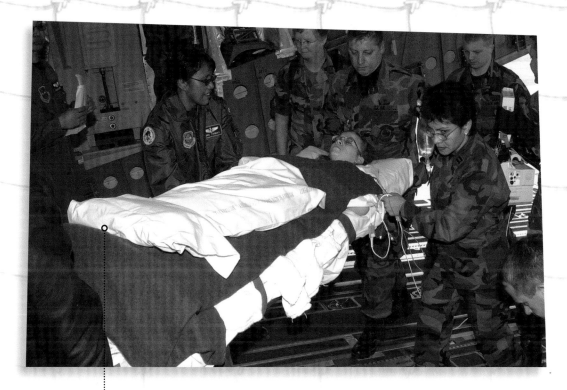

JESSICA LYNCH is carried into a US Army aircraft after her rescue.

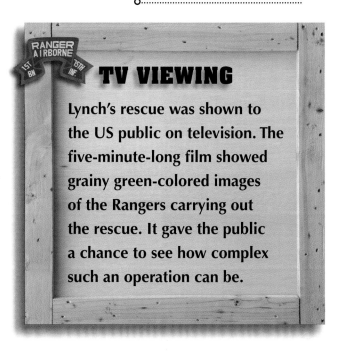

TV VIEWING

Lynch's rescue was shown to the US public on television. The five-minute-long film showed grainy green-colored images of the Rangers carrying out the rescue. It gave the public a chance to see how complex such an operation can be.

FAMOUS RESCUE

Special Forces, including US Army Rangers and Navy SEALs taken from other missions for the purpose, carried out the nighttime rescue. They used helicopters to land near the hospital and wore night-vision goggles to find their way. The Rangers and SEALs rescued Lynch and recovered the bodies of eight other Americans. It was the first successful rescue of a POW (Prisoner of War) since World War II and the first ever rescue of a female POW. The whole rescue was filmed, so everyone got to see how efficient the Special Forces were in action.

AIRCRAFT

Every Ranger is a trained parachutist. Recruits have to pass Army Jump School before they can even join the Rangers. They jump from airplanes like the C-130 Hercules. The C-130 can take off and land on unprepared runways, so it is ideal for military operations. The Rangers use different versions, including the AC-130 gunship. The aircraft has been used in Iraq and Afghanistan to provide fire cover for ground troops.

RANGERS WAIT to board a C-130 to practice a static line parachute jump.

AMC

DYESS

41689

C-17 GLOBEMASTER

The C-130 family of aircraft is quite old. A more recent addition to the Rangers' airplane complement is the C-17 Globemaster. It is a large aircraft that is capable of transporting up to 134 troops as well as heavy vehicles such as the M1 Abrams tank. The C-17 is now mainly used for the strategic airlift of troops and cargo into main operational bases. But when necessary it can also be used in more tactical operations closer to the front line. It can be turned into a mobile hospital or be used to drop Rangers into a combat zone by parachute.

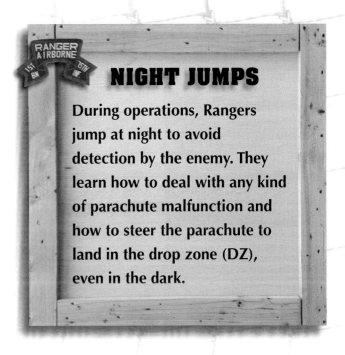

NIGHT JUMPS

During operations, Rangers jump at night to avoid detection by the enemy. They learn how to deal with any kind of parachute malfunction and how to steer the parachute to land in the drop zone (DZ), even in the dark.

RANGERS PARACHUTE
from a C-17 Globemaster III during an exercise.

HELICOPTERS

RANGERS JUMP from an MH-6 Little Bird, used for short-range patrols.

The helicopter is at the heart of most Ranger missions. The CH-47 Chinook is a twin-rotor, multifunction chopper that comes in a number of versions. The MH-47E variant is a heavy assault helicopter that can carry up to 44 soldiers. It is fitted with the latest technology, including infrared sensors and all-terrain-following radar, so it can operate below 100 feet (30 m), in bad weather, and at night.

FLYING GUNSHIPS

The other helicopter used regularly by the Rangers is the UH-60 Black Hawk. Black Hawks were used both in the Battle of Mogadishu (1993) and the rescue mission on Takur Ghar in Afghanistan (2002). The Black Hawk can carry up to 11 Rangers and can be fitted with machine guns for defense. In earlier combats, like the Vietnam War, the twin-engined UH-1 Huey had many functions. It was used for transport, as an air ambulance, for search and rescue, and as a gunship.

EYEWITNESS

"The trip to Rach Kien was by helicopter in the beloved Huey that was the workhorse of Vietnam. The ground beneath me was frequently pockmarked by bomb craters, giving it the look of a lunar landscape."

Colonel Robert W. Black
8th Airborne Ranger Company

A CHINOOK MH-47 equipped with a probe for aerial refueling makes a nighttime landing at a US base in Afghanistan.

SPECIAL GEAR

Rangers believe that their most special piece of equipment is a fully-trained Ranger. As a light infantry and airborne force, Rangers carry the minimal amount of gear they need to cover every possible outcome of an operation. Because they usually drop into a combat zone in the dark, they all have night goggles that help enhance the available light. Rangers also wear day goggles. They are trained to fight in gas masks, so they are prepared for chemical warfare.

RANGER SPECIAL Operations Vehicles (RSOVs) can carry up to seven Rangers.

RUNNING SONG

The Rangers have a cadence they chant as they run that sums up their most important weapon: themselves.

"My mind's a computer,
My fists are like steel,
If one doesn't get ya,
The other one will."

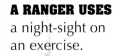

A RANGER USES a night-sight on an exercise.

THIS RANGER Special Operations Vehicle has a machine gun mounted on the top.

LOAD BEARERS

Strapped over their BDU (battledress uniform), Rangers wear a wide green belt with suspenders; this is known as their LBE (Load Bearing Equipment). It is used to carry canteens, ammo pouches, knives, first aid pouches, and flashlights. One of the most useful things Rangers can carry is a piece of strong nylon cord. It might be cut from the strings of a parachute after a jump or even bought from a hardware store, but it has lots of uses on a mission. For example, it can even be used to improvise a river crossing if necessary.

WEAPONS

Rangers carry an assortment of weapons. Training camp and Rogers' Rules teach them just how essential it is to take care of their guns. They have to learn how to disassemble and reassemble their M-16 rifles in just three minutes. To pass their marksmanship course, they must be able to hit a stationary target at 100 feet (30 m).

RANGERS ARE well camouflaged as they advance toward a target.

BOMBS AND GRENADES

In combat, the Rangers use different weapons for different situations. They use C4 explosives to destroy doors, walls, and vehicles as they enter a combat zone. Rangers carry up to 12 different types of hand grenades; the most common is the M67 fragmentation grenade. Grenades can be thrown if the enemy is within 100 feet (30 m) or fired from a grenade launcher. The M203 40mm launcher is mounted on the M-16 rifle and is accurate up to 330 feet (100 m). Rangers also carry knives for close-combat fighting.

RANGERS FIRE A Javelin missile, which can be used to attack enemy armor and buildings.

RANGERS ARE instructed in firing the Squad Automatic Weapon (SAW).

EYEWITNESS

"As we threaded our way through the narrow street with two- and three-story buildings on both sides, bullets were flying our way from every direction. We fought back with everything we had: our personal M-16s, submachine guns…"

Captain Jeff Struecker
75th Rangers,
Battle of Mogadishu

GLOSSARY

battalion (buh-TAL-yun) A large military unit made up of smaller units.

colonists (KAH-luh-nists) People who come from and are governed by another country.

commandos (kuh-MAN-dohz) A military unit trained for hit-and-run missions in enemy territory.

creed (KREED) A set of basic beliefs that someone lives by.

demilitarized zone (dih-MIH-lih-tuh-ryzd ZOHN) An area between two countries where it is forbidden for soldiers to go.

guerrilla (guh-RIL-uh) Someone who fights using ambushes and sabotage, rather than traditional battle tactics.

gunship (GUN-ship) A heavily armed airplane or helicopter.

Humvee (hum-VEE) A high-mobility military vehicle.

insurgents (in-SER-jintz) Forces who fight an established government, often by using guerrilla tactics.

patrol (puh-TROHL) A small expedition made to gather information.

rappel (ruh-PEHL) To descend quickly by sliding down a rope, using friction to stop.

reconnaissance (rih-KAH-nih-zents) Learning about the enemy's positions and strength.

scout (SCOWT) A soldier who makes reconnaissance patrols in enemy territory.

static line (STA-tik-LYN) A cord that opens a parachute when a jumper leaves a plane.

strategic (struh-TEE-jik) Relating to an overall campaign or war, rather than to individual events or battles.

surveillance (sur-VAY-lints) Secretly keeping watch on enemy movements.

volunteer (vah-lun-TEER) Someone who offers to do a duty he does not have to do.

warlord (WOR-lord) A local leader whose power is based on armed followers.

FURTHER READING

Besel, Jennifer M. *The Army Rangers.* First Facts. Mankato, MN: Capstone Press, 2011.

Samuels, Charlie. *Timeline of World War II: Pacific.* Americans at War: A Gareth Stevens Timeline Series. New York: Gareth Stevens, 2012.

Sandler, Michael. *Army Rangers in Action.* Special Ops. New York: Bearport Publishing, 2008.

Schemenauer, Elma. *Welcome to Somalia.* Welcome to the World. Mankato, MN: Child's World, 2008.

WEBSITES

Due to the changing nature of Internet links. PowerKids Press has developed an online list of websites related to the subject of this book. This site is updated regularly. Please use this link to access the list:
www.powerkidslinks.com/usf/armyr/

INDEX